All You Want To Know

About Open Data

Maria SASHINSKAYA

Brussels, 2015

All You Want To Know About Open Data

ISBN-13: 978-1542893961

ISBN-10: 1542893968

Abstract: Open data is information which is produced, collected and stored by governmental and public service bodies. It is meant to be freely available online for other stakeholders such as citizens, public organizations and business structures.

The amount of academic literature on open data topic is limited as the concept is relatively new. This book is an attempt to collect, analyze and present the current status of open data.

Disclaimer: This book is an updated chapter of the other book of the author, and covers only the topic of Open Data and public sector information (PSI). If you are interested in issues of "Smart Cities" and "Smart Mobility" as well as the role of PSI in the European Union, you might consider checking the full text of the research, available in the book **"Smart Cities in Europe - Open Data in a Smart Mobility context"**.

Table of Contents

What is Open Data?

The number of countries around the globe that put the "Open Data" concept on its political and administrative agenda is increasing significantly. Most of the time, authorities implement open data strategies to increase transparency, citizen participation and government performance efficiency.[1] Big organizations like OECD (Organization for Economic Co-operation and Development)[2], and UNESCO [3]also have started to promote open access to information and knowledge. Even though in case of UNESCO it is mostly about the right to access scientific information, the main idea of *"Open access is about Freedom, Flexibility and Fairness"* [4]can be borrowed for all the open data types.

Although the portal with public sector information datasets was launched quite recently in 2009[5], the US federal government initiative on increasing public access to governmental information can be treated as a flagman of the initiative around the globe, On his first working day as the United States President in January 2009, Barack Obama announced that his team would start a transparent open government strategy: *"We will work together to ensure the public trust and establish a system of transparency, public participation, and collaboration. Openness will strengthen our democracy and promote efficiency and effectiveness in Government."* [6]

In this perspective, the European Union has slightly longer history of dealing with open data. The first attempts have been made in 2003 with launching pan-European Directive on public sector information re-use or shortly - PSI-Directive. [7] The Commissioner responsible for the Digital Agenda implementation, Neelie Kroes accentuated the idea that nowadays data is a kind of new fuel: *"Data is new oil for a digital era".*[8] Thus, by opening up governmental data it is possible to provide stakeholders with an amount of new economical, political and social values, needed to the EU modern society. Nowadays, the website of the European Union [9] is one of the biggest web recourses in the world. It contains and at the same time gives access to more than 6 million pages of all types of information and legislative acts of the EU. [10] Thus, many essential data already exist in digital format, and still governments constantly continue to generate new amounts of data. [11] [12] Nevertheless, different authorities in different countries have their special views, motivations and official positions whether they make their PSI available or not. Even if some data are available, it's up to a national authority which terms and conditions implement to information be reused: from completely open access to limited or charged access.[13]

Anyhow, while the amount of any kinds of digital information, from mapping, social statistics and weather forecasting to private companies monitoring, is growing, public bodies have to find solutions how to maintain all this structured and unstructured data at least for their own internal needs and for the needs of society and business as well. [14] [15]

A widespread and commonly accepted argument for implementing open data strategies is that opening-up of governmental data in a reusable format can strengthen citizen engagement and force businesses to innovate. However, the open data phenomenon is relatively new and evidence of an expected positive impact still needs to be proven in more detail. Moreover, the idea of opening-up and re-using public sector information is not a neutral one. Some researchers are biased, arguing that radical openness may result in unpleasant accidents and an even further lack of trust to the government. [16] [17] Nevertheless, in this book we are not going to evaluate positive or negative impact of re-using public sector information in a deep way, as we believe it's the topic of a separate academic research. Instead, we would like to look at the phenomenon in a nutshell, to give some definitions, characteristics, types and legal basis of open data initiatives with mandatory providing the research with some essential critics on the topic.

Giving definitions to Open Data

For some reasons the amount of academic literature on open data topic is quite limited. Probably it refers to relative novelty of the concept. Giving many diverse definitions of this practice is therefore almost unfeasible at this moment. Thus, we will refer to descriptions which can be found in works of independent researchers and public open data activists. First of all, it's interesting to look at the definition which Open Knowledge Foundation[18]- the main organization advocating for opening-up governmental data around the globe - gives:

"Open data – data which is able to be used for any purpose;

Public Sector Information (PSI) – information collected or controlled by the public sector;

Open Government Data – open data produced by the government. This is generally accepted to be data gathered during the course of business as usual activities which do not identify individuals

11

or breach commercial sensitivity. Open government data is a subset of Public Sector Information, which is broader in scope".[19]

We strongly believe that the meaning of "Public Sector Information" (PSI) shouldn't be mixed up with the meaning of "open data". They are not necessarily synonyms in cases when PSI is stored by government and not opened up for the other stakeholders as citizens, commercial and non-commercial organizations. Anyhow, PSI and open data definitions can overlap and even be identical in situations where public sector information is under the open access. For example, if government collects and stores some transport or traffic congestions data, these information is PSI, because it's *"information collected or controlled by the public sector"* and obviously it's done on taxpayers' money. These information can become an "open data" only when it is announced, published and *"able to be used for any purpose"*. Any non-governmental entity can also make its private information open for a public and make it "open data". It basically means, that "open data" is not necessarily governmental data either. Thus, these two types of information (PSI and open data) are not automatically the same things, even though in some cases we can talk about PSI as a form of open data.

In the report for the European Commission on the topic of commercial exploitation of PSI, Public Sector Information is defined as *"...information created, collected, developed and disseminated by the public sector"* [20]

The other Commission definition on open public data is following: *"Public data is all the information that public bodies in the European Union produce, collect or pay for. This could include geographical data, statistics, meteorological data, data from publicly funded research projects, and digitised books from libraries"*. [21]

The author of the open data best practices research, Marco Fioretti, also identifies PSI as *"data that is of public interest, that belongs to the whole community, data that every citizen is surely entitled to know and use"*. [22]

In other words, collecting all this definitions and extracting the most important ideas out of it, we can define open data and open PSI as ***information which is produced, collected and stored by governmental and public service bodies. It is meant to be freely available on-***

line for other stakeholders such as citizens, public organizations and business structures.

Furthermore it's important to mention that data should be collected, stored and presented in a digital form, even if initially it was generated in a traditional paper way. From the moment datasets have been digitalized, they can be disseminated and new data can be built on its basis. [23]

Open Data classification

Fioretti[24] gives some typology of open data, which we find the most comprehensive and clear classification at the moment. By adding some European Commission descriptions and clarifications[25], we can present fairly complete, in our opinion, the typology of open data.

<u>Types of Open data with examples</u>:

• Geographical and Local transportation data (maps, land exploitation, cadastre information, addresses, public transport schedules and real-time performance, street cameras images, traffic data etc.)

• Demographic data (age and sex information about city inhabitants, birth and death statistics etc.)

• Election data (activity of the local administration members, their everyday work statistics and voting preferences on each relevant city topic, law proposals statuses etc.)

- Budgets and taxes data (salaries of public authorities, local budget lines spending)

- Security and legal data (crime statistics, police performances, law enforcement)

- Local activities data (location and contact information of the public and private services)

- Real Estate data (household locations, apartment's prices, time traveling from one household to another or to a public service body etc.)

- Energy and water production and consumption data (energy and water consumption data from citizens, public bodies and industry)

- Environmental data and pollution measurements (air, water and land pollution rates, possible harmful emissions from industrial sector or public and private transport)

- Waste and water management data (garbage collection schedules for each neighborhood, amount of water wasting, how much money spent on it etc.)

- Health-related data (hospital performances, spread of infections)

- Education data (school locations and costs, student grades performances in every school, sex and average age of students, available resources as libraries and gyms etc.)

- Agricultural and fisheries data (crop fields areas, the number of fish caught per year etc.)

- Scientific data (research of the universities, publicly-funded research institutes, patents information etc.).

- Cultural data (materials of museums, art galleries, exhibitions, festivals, library resources etc.)

Apparently, the value of any type of PSI is increasing exponentially when it can be combined and linked with other data. For example, a family can make a decision to move to another city. Geographical and public transport data can be combined with real estate data and security and crime statistics to choose a better neighborhood for living. Energy and water consumption data combined with health and education data can help in planning the family budget. And finally, cultural and election data can give them an idea what the community looks like, which values and priorities are shared by neighbors and local administration. This complex of open data can give to a family, which decided to live in a new city, a holistic picture of a new living place and make possible expectations more or less objective from the very beginning.

Nevertheless, we believe that the list of open data types can be longer and probably will expand due to new open datasets.

What is real "openness"?

To call data "open" we should distinguish a number of characteristics, which can make particular information open. Peter Murray-Rust, a chemist from Cambridge Center of Molecular informatics, who is currently working on issues of general "openness" of information, presents some universal conditions for open data.[26]

First of all, according to the scientist, the fundamental rule of any open information is its possibility to be re-used because any barrier to this process can damage a semantic value of data. Among other conditions of "openness", Peter Murray-Rust also argues to abilities of data to be redistributed, attributed, integrated and not to be discriminated against persons, groups and fields of endeavor including any commercial using. According to the author of the classification, all the conditions are mandatory and none of them can be optional.

The other system of "openness" evaluation is less strict and rather flexible. In 2010 the Director of the World

Wide Web Consortium, Tim Bernes-Lee, proposed a "5-star system for open data". [27] This rating system is aimed to help public sector bodies to work on opening-up their data.

Number of stars	Meaning
no stars	Information is available on-line, but not available to be re-used under an open license
1 star	Information is available on-line under an open license, but understandable only for a human eye (text format)
2 stars	Information is available on-line under an open license, structured and available for machines (Excel format)
3 stars	Information is available on-line under an open license,

	structured and available for machines (no dependency on a particular software producer)
4 stars	Information is available on-line under an open license, structured, available for machines and has it's unique URI (Uniform Resource Identifier)
5 stars	Information is available on-line under an open license, structured, available for machines, has it's unique URI and can be linked and interconnected to other data using network effects and creating new value

Five-star system for open data

Berners-Lee, T. (2010) Speech on "Open, Linked Data for a Global Community", Gov 2.0 Expo 2010.

The main idea of this "5-star system for open data" is to show that public data can be completely useful only if it has an ability to be linked with other data sets and create new social and economical value. Thus, **interoperability** is a crucial issue in the open data discourse. This universal characteristic allows different components of complex systems to work together. We can even compare the nature of interoperability with a common technological language. Anyway, an interoperability can be defined as "a result of mixing data and pieces of content from different sources and re-using it in unexpected ways" [28]

Going back to the Cambridge scientist Peter Murray-Rust thoughts on open data, it seems evident that some of public authorities' on-line resources, which are positioning themselves as "open", are not really that open. According to the scientist, it can be judged by several parameters:[29]

- only part of data are available

- there are limits to the amount of downloaded data

- re-use is forbidden because of copyrights to the information

- data are not marked as open (through open licenses) and thus, the possibility to use it is vague

Therefore, at this stage of open data initiatives implementations, we can talk about existing division between "complete openness" and "selective openness" approaches. Obviously "something" is always better than "nothing" and the process of opening-up and re-using of PSI has started recently. More attention to it should be given and more work should be done by public sector bodies around the globe and in the EU in particular.

Governmental motivations to open-up its data

The idea behind the open data concept is quite simple. First of all, the right to knowledge is a basic principle of democracy, and if a government is ready to become transparent and innovative, all the public value data should be easily accessible for citizens (whether it's state spending reports, pollution rates or public transport data).

Moreover, citizens have already paid from their taxes for collecting and storing all this huge amount of data and now these data can and should be re-used for their benefits and even by themselves.

Some researches even emphasize that keeping data closed is much more expensive than putting it online. [30] So, if data are still being collected, what to do with all this information and how can it really make the choice of citizens wider and the governmental work more effective? In this respect the researchers of the open data phenomenon distinguish three primary motivations for a government to create open data strategies[31]:

24

- Increasing democratic control and political participation of citizens;

- Pushing law enforcement;

- Fostering services and products innovations

First of all, launching of a big amount of datasets can increase democratic control and political participation of citizens: *"Open Data transform not just the way services are delivered but, more importantly, allow citizens to control those services."* [32] Perhaps, without the Internet broad transparency would be unfeasible and much more expensive. Curtin and Meijer say that the Internet is a significant platform and at the same time a driver for transparency. [33] Basically, if the information is open and the more people can have free access to it, the more reasons for a government to be crystal clear by performing a public task. On the other hand, some researches argue that opening-up data is not a guarantee for a government to be transparent: *"There is no automatic cause-effect relationship between Open Data and real transparency and democracy. On the contrary, several problems may occur, if administrators and citizens don't pay close attention".* [34] Later on in this Chapter we will look through possible negative effects of open data in more detail.

Second possible reason for governments to open their data, and we believe this motive is linked with the first one (transparency), is pushing a law enforcement and involving citizens in legislation monitoring. [35]City crime statistics and budget spending can be examples of this issue. Obviously, here a government is becoming closer to citizens by opening up and sharing its significant and quite delicate information.

Finally, the third primer motive for a government to create open data strategies (and we believe this motive could be probably the most promising in the digital age), is fostering services and products innovations. [36] Talking about the open data phenomenon it's important to mention that the interest of local and national authorities can be stimulated not only by internal reasons of transparency and public loyalty, but also by external motives as technologies development and local business interests. Reasonable to say, the rise of the social networks and increasing role of mobile Internet in everyday life encourages businesses to the creation of new services based on the government data.

Collecting, analyzing and using data can be beneficial to non-governmental sectors. In fact, the wide range of open data sets can potentially encourage businesses to find a way to make profit out of re-using PSI and innovate in a private sector. If we go back to our attempts to explain the Smart City concept and remind the idea of "government is a platform", we will also investigate that the authors believe that the most successful platforms are open platforms because the power of open standards is cultivates innovation. The logic is simple: if it's easy for an entrepreneur to enter the market - the innovation goes natural and free, instead *"when barriers are high, innovation moves elsewhere"*. [37] Moreover, according the other group of authors, the main advantage of open data is exactly in the fact that the nature of openness works both ways: for the transparency and for the innovation, because developers very often re-use data in really unexpected and very creative ways. The Economist magazine also agrees with the idea that the potential of PSI is yet not explored till the end: "The data-centered economy is just nascent". [38]

Taking into account these tree basic motivations for a modern government, obviously, open data recourses can become a natural advantage of smart cities.[39] When we say that open data recourses are a natural advantage, we also refer to the pre-paid character of this information. The information is already collected and stored by local and pan-European authorities. It means that for this re-using no big amount of money is needed (except if there is the need to transform public sector information data into machine-readable formats and putting it on special on-line portals). A city already has statistical data recourses and the recourse itself is quite natural for the territory in terms of governmental effort to get it.

Critics of Open Data concept

Many world governments nowadays have open data programs. Some of the strategies are quite successful and effective in opening-up datasets, others – not even trying to improve the level of "openness", preferring to have programs only on paper.

Fioretti is wondering: *"If openness is so good, why aren't all Public Data already open?"*[40] Indeed, the question is rational and the author is trying to find the answer, arguing to different reasons from lack of sustainable physical infrastructures and Internet connections to abridging the freedom of speech.

Among others, the author distinguishes further reasons why some governments are not very active in opening-up their data sets:

- Lack of legal framework, legal barriers and copyright law domination

- Lack of awareness and guiding about potential benefits of PSI re-use

- Biases against security issues

- Unwillingness to publish low quality and inaccurate data

- Lack of funds to transform data into machine-readable format and/or to publish it

To be objective and make our research balanced we find it necessary to indicate and systematize possible controversial issues of open data, the reasons for governments to stop implementing open data strategies.

- First of all, a clear definition of PSI and open data is needed.

Is PSI can be all the information produced by governments and public bodies? In fact, city administrations are normally also responsible for monitoring activities of private companies. Can this still be considered as PSI in case of anonymization statistical data or should this issue be protected under the privacy law?[41] What if published data is inaccurate or not up-to-date?

Imagine a traffic management application based on this data – it can be a cause of even more congestion on certain roads.

- Not only inaccurate, but also intentionally manipulated data can be potentially published by public bodies.

As long as people trust official information and don't verify or double check it[42], the risk that data is manipulated can even decrease the trust in the government. Thus, stakeholders and users should still think critically about where data comes from and through/with which principles it was collected. [43] Some open data sets, together with proper analytics, can make people prejudged.

For example, it's quite delicate to open up statistics of which district in the city is the most polluted or which part of the city has the highest crime rate, because people simply can start trying to avoid these places. Again, what if the data in this case is not accurate?

- There is a common threat that some people can exploit PSI in a wrong or illegal way.

For example, opening up a map of public toilets can provoke perverts activity. In this discourse we would like to use a clear example which the Canadian open government activist David Eaves gives in his blog.[44] When a government builds a road, this road potentially can be used by both – a robber, who can run away from police through this road and for an ambulance car, which takes the road to save someone's life. Should a government reject the idea to build a new road only because it can be potentially used for illegal actions? As a result: instead of rejecting the idea of opening-up PSI, a legal framework for dealing with open data crimes should be better developed.

- One more thing which should be developed in a legal frame work is the question of licensing open data.

In some cases governments publish data on-line, but under a copyright or "all rights reserved", which by default prohibits any further re-use of these information.[45] Licensing procedures should be adjusted for easy data exchange between stakeholders – business and public bodies (member states in the EU particular case).

• It's still an issue when public bodies publish their data in text or any other non-machine readable format.

In these cases formally data are open, but not prepared for re-use, which makes interoperability an issue. Reasonable question is also: who needs to transform these data into a machine readable format and provide access to it? From which budget should it be paid? Should the requirement of publishing data in machine readable format be implemented only to new data sets or does this also apply for previously published data?

• There is a common idea, that open data is mainly beneficial for big service corporations that know how to monetize the information rather than for ordinary citizens, who can even be indifferent to these governmental initiatives.[46] [47]

33

- Linked to the previous issue, this lack of interest from ordinary citizens can make PSI available only to upper classes of society - people, who have better Internet access, modern digital devices and more skills in using online services.

In other words, open data can be one of the reasons of digital exclusion rather than making life of citizens more comfortable. Thus, unequal access and lack of skills and interest to PSI will not bring any effect to this initiative.

- The economic impact of open data strategies implementation still remains vague.[48]

As in every innovative situation it's hard to model possible social and economic outcomes, especially if it concerns so many different countries and cities. What works for one place doesn't necessarily fit another place. Also here the question could be raised: should PSI be free of charge for citizens and business or does a government have the right to earn on it or at least cover some marginal costs? According to the Canadian experience, PSI should be free of charge: *"...the total value of public data is maximized when provided for free or where necessary only a minimal cost of distribution ... and when data is shared freely, citizens are enabled to use and re-purpose it to help create a more economically vibrant and environmentally sustainable city"[49].* The US researchers agree: *"When public sector bodies charge for PSI, those costs can actually inhibit others from adding value. The same is true with licensing restrictions"[50].* On the other hand, we can look at the issue from a governmental perspective, which should find money to publish, maintain and up-date PSI data on-line preferably in machine readable formats. Again it's the tax payer who is covering all these cost to finally enable businesses the chance to make profit out of re-use.

Summary and Conclusions

PSI (public sector information) is data naturally collected and stored by government. Some countries' and cities' authorities make a decision to open it up and let the third parties to use it. Then PSI is becoming an open data. Even though these two concepts (open data and PSI) are not the same things in its cores, in some cases open data and PSI tend to be overlapping notions.

Open Data is a global trend at the moment. More and more governmental bodies and international organizations are interested in opening-up their datasets to get some social and economical benefits out of it. Produced, collected and stored by governmental and public service bodies information are expected to be freely available on-line for other stakeholders as citizens, public organizations and business structures. However, sometimes the matters of interoperability, licensing and structuring datasets becomes difficult. As a result, not all the open data are purely "open".

In spite of some disputable issues around PSI and controversial moments of its re-use, there are some significant motives for local authorities to open-up their data, mainly in terms of increasing citizen transparency and fostering innovations. Obviously, in every individual city case risks should be measured and balanced with possible benefits. In fact, this "balance point searching" can be the topic of another big research on the concept of "open data".

Open Data.

The legal framework overview

National policy makers are important drivers for open data initiatives development and the process of motivating people to use open data and PSI[51]. Moreover, the lack of political leadership and initiatives to PSI re-use is exactly the reason for the existing blockage of the progress on open data policy. Thus, we find it necessary to make an overview of the current policy framework regarding the PSI domain.

This part of our research is extremely important because it explains indirectly why some cities are "smarter" and more mobile than others. In some territories the implementation of the European legislation on open data goes coherently and with strong support of local authorities. The effect of such a *willingness to open* is relatively visible and reflected in launching of new paid and free services in the market (for example: the number of diverse mobile apps for public transport, built on open governmental data). On the contrary, other EU member states are less flexible and even slow in transposing pan-European legislation into their national legal frameworks.

Nevertheless, in this Chapter we are not going to speculate and find out the reasons why some European countries are faster and more flexible than others. Our aim is to make an overview of the legitimate open data framework in order to understand the legal basis of this approach.

International framework. OECD - Principles and Guidelines for Access to Research Data from Public Funding (2007)

The first and probably the most general document we want to look at is OECD's (Organization for Economic Co-operation and Development) paper called "Principles and Guidelines for Access to Research Data from Public Funding".

In 2004 in Paris the Organization for Economic Co-operation and Development, consisting of 34 country members (24 out of which are European countries), together with China, Israel, Russia and South Africa adopted a Declaration on Access to Research Data from Public Funding.[52] The paper recognizes the importance of free public access to all publicly-funded archive data. Later on, in 2006-2007 the OECD also developed and published the Principles and Guidelines for Access to Research Data from Public Funding. [53]

Basically, the paper is recognizing the importance of free public access to all publicly-funded archive data and its main idea can be formulated as: *"The exchange of ideas, knowledge and data emerging is fundamental for human progress and is part of the core of OECD values".*[54]

The document is based on 13 main principles[55], which are:

- Openness
- Flexibility
- Transparency
- Legal conformity
- Protection of intellectual property
- Formal responsibility
- Professionalism
- Interoperability
- Quality
- Security
- Efficiency
- Accountability
- Sustainability

Moreover, it's emphasized several times in the paper that **data should be digital and interoperable** (*"preferably data should be Internet-based", "ideally through the Internet", "should be easy to find on the Internet"*...etc).

The document is created in a form of recommendations and doesn't have any legal binding status. Anyway, this "soft law" paper actively encourages the OECD member countries take the principles into consideration and implement them in a long standing practice.

The document applies only to publicly-funded archive data and does not damages any privacy low or confidential information: *"Data on human subjects and other personal data are subject to restricted access under national laws and policies to protect confidentiality and privacy"*. [56] However, according to this paper, anonymisation and privacy procedures which guarantee a decent level of confidentiality can be considered to open up for researchers as much valuable data as it possible.

This intergovernmental agreement is more likely the only international document which the EU Member States (at least those who adopted the document) could take into consideration. For the other cases, we clearly can observe strong domination of the European Union legislation. Thus, the biggest part of the Chapter is going to cover this matter.

European Union framework.

Digital Agenda and public data core

Directives

Digital Agenda for Europe is a flagship initiative of the EU which was launched in August 2010 and aimed to develop a digital single market in the territory of the European Union. The main standing point of this initiative is the idea that nowadays public, governmental and commercial services are moving towards more digitalization and the Union can benefit from this tendency. Therefore, to remain competitive in the world market during a period of economical challenges and at the same time making life of European citizens more comfortable, it is necessary to work on developing new services and particularly on opening up public data.[57]

Among other initiatives declared in this document, the idea of opening up and re-using public sector information (PSI) is clearly noticeable: *"...governments can stimulate content markets by making **public sector information** available on transparent, effective, non-discriminatory terms. This is* *an important source of potential growth of innovative online services…public bodies must be obliged to open up data resources for cross-border applications and services ".[58]*

Later on Neelie Kroes, the Commissioner responsible for the Digital Agenda implementation, more than once has emphasized that opening up governmental data gives a whole new economical, political and social value to the EU society: *"Data is new oil for a digital era".[59]*

Under the umbrella of the Digital Agenda we can find several Directives, which are the basic tools for the EU authorities to implement the policy around the member states. Referring to public sector information and open data in the context of mobility initiatives we can distinguish two core directives:

1. DIRECTIVE 2003/98/EC OF THE EUROPEAN PARLIAMENT AND OF THE COUNCIL on the re-use of public sector information (of 17 November 2003)

2. DIRECTIVE 2007/2/EC OF THE EUROPEAN PARLIAMENT AND OF THE COUNCIL establishing an Infrastructure for Spatial

Information in the European Community (INSPIRE) (of 14 March 2007)

In this Chapter we would like to take a more in depth look into these two directives (shortly – PSI Directive and INSPIRE Directive) as general key drivers of the open data initiative. Its implementation status and specialties of implementation among the Member States will be covered in the next Chapters in the context of cities case studies.

DIRECTIVE 2003/98/EC OF THE EUROPEAN PARLIAMENT AND OF THE COUNCIL on the re-use of public sector information (of 17 November 2003)

Even though the document was launched in 2003, seven years earlier than the Digital Agenda, now it fits the purposes of this initiative and directly refers to the knowledge society and the importance of public sector information as a primary material for digital content products: *"The evolution towards an information and knowledge society influences the life of every citizen in the Community, inter alia, by enabling them to gain new ways of accessing and acquiring knowledge".* [60]

The Directive (also known as PSI Directive) aims to facilitate the process of re-using public sector information (PSI) in a single digital market by establishing basic re-use conditions, and providing the market with a sufficient legal frame work to do so. [61] The paper is supposed to support the establishment of an internal market, expanding the role of community-wide services in the EU economy. According to the document, data shall be re-usable for commercial or non-commercial purposes, because re-using PSI (as an important primary material for the digital industry) should contribute to the economy and as a result a social growth of the EU. The concept of public sector bodies is based on the idea of public task or *"raison d'être"* for the public sector: *"...established for the specific purpose of meeting needs in the general interest, not having an industrial or commercial character..."*[62] This is why **the idea of wasting some economic potential by not re-using public sector data is the basic idea of the document.** In other words, the EU citizens have already paid for collecting and storing all this huge amount of data from their taxes and now these data can and should be re-used for making cities "smarter" and life of its citizens more comfortable.

First of all, the Directive doesn't deal with any data protected by intellectual property rights, copyrights or any kind of national security documents, commercial confidentiality and other private information. It can be applied only to the data (paper documents or sound and audio-visual information), which regional and local governments of the member states are launching on a daily basis.[63]

According to the document, the access to re-use data should be fast (for example for traffic data), because regular up-dates influence the economic value of the usage of this information. According the Directive, as far as the information is already paid off by taxes, whenever possible PSI should be re-used by third parties free of charge or at least not more than marginal costs: *"Where charges are made, the total income from supplying and allowing re-use of documents shall not exceed the cost of collection, production, reproduction and dissemination, together with a reasonable return on investment."*[64]

In addition to this statement, the conditions of "non-discrimination" policy should be observed: *"The re-use of documents shall be open to all potential actors in the market, even if one or more market players already exploit added-value products based on these documents. Contracts or other arrangements between the public sector bodies holding the documents and third parties shall not grant exclusive rights."*[65] In other words, every public body, private company or citizen should have equal rights to get the data.

Public sector bodies should also make data available in formats, applicable for electronic needs or machine-readable: *"Where possible, documents shall be made available through electronic means."*[66]

As the main basics of the PSI Directive are "transparency and a fair competition"[67], the legal process of re-using PSI in the territory of the EU is the following: national public sector authorities process requests of stakeholders (citizens, commercial and non-commercial organizations) and make PSI available on-line preferably in machine-readable formats. In case of licensing, it should take not more than 20 days for a public body to explain to an applicant the requirements. In case it's impossible to open-up public sector body's data, this organization should give reasons why information is closed. When any payments or charges are needed to share the data, the public sector body, , shouldn't exceed marginal costs (costs of production, collection and distribution). Moreover, these charging conditions should be pre-presented and published. Thus, the competition should be non-discriminatory and the information has to be available for all the interested stakeholders under the equal rules and conditions. Exclusive arrangements are prohibited. In fact, all this primary minimum of rules can, and preferably should be expended and improved by member states, as long as the Directive sets only the minimum recommendations.

It's important to note that previously the questions of open data regulations were ruled specifically according to the member states regulation. After the entering into the force the PSI Directive on 31 December 2003, open data regulation officially became a legislative act of the European Union.

The Directive is built above the Member States rules concerning the access to information and doesn't have the purpose to damage it. In fact, it can only encourage, by a minimum set of rules, the EU member states to make public sector information available for private and public organizations as well as for citizens.

Although the PSI Directive was not fully transposed into the all Member States national legislations until 2008, it has some optimistic moves within the EU. According to some resent researches, re-use of PSI is increasing, especially in the sector of geographical information.[68]

The Directive was not fully transposed by all member states until the official deadline – 2008, but by July 2010, all 27 EU members notified the Commission about factual implementation of the PSI Directive rules into their national legislation. The next review of the PSI Directive was planned by 2012, thus in December 2011 the Commission launched a co-called "Open Data Package" which includes:

- a Communication on open data:
- a Proposal for a revision of the Directive
- new Commission rules on re-use of the documents

In June 2009 the PSI Directive was reviewed. The Commission examined the way in which the EU PSI rules had been applied. As a result, the Commission confirmed that PSI re-usage had been growing, but to use the full potential of PSI for the EU economy, EU Member States had to remove some still remaining barriers and also emphasize that the situation in the European Union is in clear contrast with the US, where re-use is strongly encouraged.[69] Hence, according to this review document, Member States should take further steps to use the whole potential of PSI for the EU economy. According to the Commission clarification, the situation in the EU is in clear contrast with the US, where re-use is strongly encouraged.[70]

In 2010 the Commission arranged some consultations with interested parties (citizens, academics, public authorities, etc.)[71] According to these consultations, the Commission concluded that people are not really supporting charging for PSI and think it should be free for non-commercial re-use. they complained that public sector information should also be accessable across the Union borders, which is fully supporting the idea of a digital single market, emphasized in the Digital Agenda. The principle when the public bodies should not be allowed to charge more than marginal costs was established and highly encouraged.

In the Legislative proposal of the document (2011), the Commission proposes co-called *"Impact assessment"*, which suggests five possible options on the PSI legislation development. [72] **The first option** assumes no policy changes, remaining the Directive the way it is. **The second option** is rather radical. It suggests discontinuing of the PSI Directive. This basically means that without this document Member States can still be free to revise their own national implementing legislation for public sector information re-use., this option could mean that it will be only the Member States themselves who are responsible for opening up and processing all the PSI on their jurisdiction without reporting to the Commission. **The third option**, which the Commission has proposed in the revision of the Directive is kind of a "soft law" measure where the EU official body can only guide and give recommendations to the Member States. This consultancy, according to the option, can concern supervision on some technical issues (for example: formats and interoperability matters) and financial issues (for example: price calculations or marginal costs estimations). **Option number four** implies lawmaking amendments which basically could turn the legislation to some new areas. As to these amendments we can refer for example an *"extension of the scope of the Directive to currently excluded sectors (cultural,* *educational and research establishments as well as public"*. Another quite visible action could be *"imposing a requirement to publish data in machine-readable formats"* [73]

The last proposed option, **option number five** is called "Packaged solution" which basically combines options #3 and #4 - guidelines and recommendations from the Commission to the Members States on technical and financial issues with some legislative amendments in terms of the current Directive extension.

According to the Legislative proposal paper, exactly option #4 offers the best balance between developing the idea of the re-using of PSI and its legal harmonization with national law specificities.

According to the Commission Communication on open data, minimum harmonization in PSI didn't resolve the problem of differences in the member states law and, as a result, development of cross-border information services. One of the biggest issues is monopolistic tendencies on open data keeping. Thus, the main conclusion is: "At the moment, its full potential is far from being realized" and more steps to opening-up public sector information should be done by both sides: the Commission and the member states.

The proposals for a revision of the Directive[74]:

• to include new PSI bodies (public and university libraries, museums and archives)
• to limit the fees for PSI re-use by the marginal costs
• to make data interoperable and machine-readable

The PSI Directive was revised in 2013.

The core of the document reminds the same, however three topics were further covered: recommended standard licenses, datasets and charging.

First of all, the usage of simple standard licenses in digital format was recommended instead of individual licenses. According to recommendations, a preference should be given to the use of open licenses such as "Creative Commons".

Five dataset categories of high priority were identified:

- Geospatial data (postcodes, national and local maps).

- Environmental data (weather, land and water quality, energy consumption, emission levels).

- Transport data (public transport timetables, road works, traffic information).

- Statistical data (GDP, age, health, unemployment, income, education, etc.).

- Selected company data (company and business registers).

The European Commission encourages the datasets owners to provide quality, interoperability and availability of data. No-cost policy is also highly recommended by the Commission. In case it is not feasible to implement, public sector bodies are advised to conduct cost-demand evaluation and adjust charges accordingly.

DIRECTIVE 2007/2/EC OF THE EUROPEAN PARLIAMENT AND OF THE COUNCIL establishing an Infrastructure for Spatial Information in the European Community (INSPIRE) (of 14 March 2007)

The INSPIRE Directive[75] was adopted by the EU on the 14th of March 2007 and entered into force on the 15th of May 2007. Full implementation of the document is required by all the Member States by 2019. The document was launched to create a pan-European spatial data infrastructure to facilitate the sharing of environmental spatial information among public sector bodies across the EU and make public access to spatial information across Europe easier.

The INSPIRE Directive doesn't deal with any data protected by intellectual property rights, copyrights or any kind of national security documents, commercial confidentiality and other private information. *"This Directive does not affect the existence or ownership of public authorities' intellectual property rights*. [76] The document can be applied only to the geo-special data, which regional and local governments of the Member States launches.

The Directive addresses 34 spatial data themes[77] needed for environmental applications (geology, transport networks, area management, utility governmental services etc.) and in a particular refers to air, water, soil and natural landscape data.

The main idea of the paper is that the infrastructure for spatial data should be established on pan-European level. Thus, in all the member states spatial data should be collected, stored, maintained and made available in the most appropriate way to use it across the EU. In addition, member states should provide data through the EU with the help of a special INSPIRE geo-portal operated by the Commission.

Taking into account regional and local differences and situations in different Member States of the EU, the coordination between them is needed. Thus, formats and the structure of the data should be interoperable and based on the international standards. To provide Member States with tools for interoperability, the document proposes to establish a special web-site, geoportal: *"The Commission shall establish and operate an Inspire geoportal at Community level"* [78]

A lot of attention is paid to the importance of making the data interoperable, because the main purpose of the initiative is smooth using all this data across the EU: *" ... 'interoperability' means the possibility for spatial data sets to be combined, and for services to interact, without repetitive manual intervention, in such a way that the result is coherent and the added value of the data sets and services is enhanced...*"[79] or *"...organisations established under international law have adopted relevant standards to ensure interoperability or harmonisation of spatial data sets and services, these standards shall be integrated..."*[80]

according to the document, the minimum number of services should be available free of charge: *"Member States shall ensure that the services referred to in points (a) and (b) of Article 11(1) are available to the public free of charge"*[81] in spite of it *"This Directive does not require collection of new spatial data".*[82]

In fact, the INSPIRE Directive is aimed to assist some policy-making process in issues of spatial information services across Europe, but also this document has a clear potential for smart cities development. Based on open air, water, soil and natural landscape data the Member States governments and pan-European organizations have the ability to create new diverse environmental applications concerning transport networks, area management, geology issues, utility governmental services etc.

Correspondence of two Directives

The Commission invites the EU Member States to adopt "re-use" and "geo-spatial data" sharing policies as early as possible. Hence, some countries are not in a hurry while others have launched their own programs under these two Directives to implement the documents smoothly. A more in depth view on these specific governmental initiatives is provided in the case studies Chapter of this paper.

Going back to two basic public data Directives (PSI Directive and INSPIRE Directive) it seems essential to say some words about the way these documents correspond to each other. First of all, **both papers argue that the right to knowledge is a basic principle of democracy, so public data should be open for easy access to citizens**. Secondly, the importance of opening up data for economical reasons is highly emphasized in the PSI Directive while the importance of interoperability of data is more covered in the INSPIRE Directive text. At the same time, both directives actively promote the idea of re-using and sharing data free of charge or at least not exceeding the marginal costs.

Summary and Conclusions

To understand the process of open data initiative implementation and evaluate the results of this approach in different EU Member States, we first should look at the legal framework of the issue in all the possible levels: from global, through the EU down to the national Member States.

The PSI Directive and INSPIRE Directive are general key drivers of open data initiatives in the European Union. Even though these two documents have different primary motivations, both papers support the idea of re-using and sharing data free of charge or at least not exceeding the marginal costs. The PSI Directive is mainly based on economic reasons and the potential values of re-using public sector information for the Member States economy, while the INSPIRE Directive promotes the significance of interoperability of data within the EU. According to both documents, re-using of public data is a basis for a digital age, thus data shall be re-usable and interoperable across the EU borders.

If you are interested in "Smart Cities" and "Smart Mobility" topics as well as the role of open data in the European Union, you might consider checking the other book of the author, **"Smart Cities in Europe - Open Data in a Smart Mobility context"**.

Bibliography

[1] Huijboom, N. & T. Van den Broek (2011) "Open data: an international comparison of strategies", *European Journal of ePractice,* 12 (March/April 2011), pp. 4-15. Available online:
http://www.epractice.eu/files/European%20Journal%20epractice%20Volume%2012_4.pdf (Last retrieved 15/08/2012)

[2] OECD (2007) "Principles and Guidelines for Access to Research Data from Public Funding" Available online: http://www.oecd.org/science/scienceandtechnologypolicy/38500813.pdf (Last retrieved 21/09/2012)

[3] Swan, A. (2012) "Policy Guidelines for the Development and Promotion of Open Access", *Published by the United Nations Educational, Scientific and Cultural Organization – UNESCO.* Available online:
http://unesdoc.unesco.org/images/0021/002158/215863e.pdf (Last retrieved 21/09/2012)

[4] Swan, A. (2012) "Policy Guidelines for the Development and Promotion of Open Access", *Published by the United Nations Educational, Scientific and Cultural Organization – UNESCO,* pp. 6-12. Available online:
http://unesdoc.unesco.org/images/0021/002158/215863e.pdf (Last retrieved 21/09/2012)

[5] The US Federal Government open data web portal: http://www.data.gov/ (Last retrieved 15/10/2012)

[6] Obama, B. (2009) "Memorandum for the Heads of Executive Departments and Agencies: Transparency and Open Government". Available online: http://www.whitehouse.gov/the_press_office/TransparencyandOpenGovernment

(Last retrieved 29/09/2012)

[7] EUROPEAN PARLIAMENT & COUNCIL (2003) Directive 2003/98/EC of the European Parliament and the Council of 17 November 2003, on the re-use of public sector information.

[8] Kroes, N. (2012) Speech on ePSI conference in Rotterdam March 2012. Available online: http://www.youtube.com/watch?v=9Jq4Qy1UeAE (Last retrieved 03/11/2012)

[9] The official website of the European Union. Available online: http://europa.eu/ (Last retrieved 15/10/2012)

[10] Curtin, D.& A. Meijer (2006) "Does Transparency Strengthen Legitimacy? A Critical Analysis of European Union Policy Documents", *Information Polity*, 11(2006), pp. 109-122.

[11] Uhlir, P.F. (2009) "The Socioeconomic Effects of Public Sector Information on Digital Networks: Toward a Better Understanding of Different Access and Reuse Policies: Workshop Summary", *US National Committee CODATA, in cooperation with OECD*, pp. 25-39.

[12] Fioretti, M. (2011)" Open Data: Emerging trends, issues and best practices", *Laboratory of Economics and Management of Scuola Superiore Sant'Anna*, Pisa, pp. 3-7.

[13] Uhlir, P.F. (2009) "The Socioeconomic Effects of Public Sector Information on Digital Networks: Toward a Better Understanding of Different Access and Reuse Policies: Workshop Summary", *US National Committee CODATA, in cooperation with OECD*, pp. 9-24.

[14] Fioretti, M. (2011)" Open Data: Emerging trends, issues and best practices", *Laboratory of Economics and Management of Scuola Superiore Sant'Anna*, Pisa, pp. 5-15.

[15] Directorate General for the Information Society (2000) Commercial Exploitation of Europe's Public Sector Information: Final Report. Available online: http://ec.europa.eu/information_society/policy/psi/docs/pdfs/p ira_study/commercial_final_report.pdf (Last retrieved

05/07/2012)

[16] Fioretti, M. (2011)" Open Data: Emerging trends, issues and best practices", *Laboratory of Economics and Management of Scuola Superiore Sant'Anna*, Pisa, pp. 3-27.

[17] Dutra, M. (2011) Dangers of Open Government Data, *The Networked Society Blog.* Retrieved from: http://thenetworkedsociety.blogspot.be/2011/03/dangers-of-open-government-data.html

[18] The official website of the Open Knowledge Foundation. Available online: http://okfn.org/ (Last retrieved 01/10/2012)

[19] Open Knowledge Foundation (2012) Open Data Handbook. Available online: http://opendatahandbook.org/en/glossary.html#term-public-sector-information (Last retrieved 01/10/2012)

[20] Directorate General for the Information Society (2000) Commercial Exploitation of Europe's Public Sector Information: Final Report, pp. 8-14. Available online: http://ec.europa.eu/information_society/policy/psi/docs/pdfs/pira_study/commercial_final_report.pdf (Last retrieved 05/07/2012)

[21] The official website of the European Union (2012) Digital Agenda: Commission's Open Data Strategy, Questions & answers. Available online: http://europa.eu/rapid/press-release_MEMO-11-891_en.htm?locale=en (Last retrieved 13/08/2012)

[22] Fioretti, M. (2011)" Open Data: Emerging trends, issues and best practices", *Laboratory of Economics and Management of Scuola Superiore Sant'Anna*, Pisa, pp. 3-27

[23] Murray-Rust, P. (2012) BioIT 2009 – What is data? *Personal blog on open knowledge.* Available online:

http://blogs.ch.cam.ac.uk/pmr/2009/04/29/bioit-2009-what-is-data-1/ (Last retrieved 04/11/2012)

[24] Fioretti, M. (2011)" Open Data: Emerging trends, issues and best practices", *Laboratory of Economics and Management of Scuola Superiore Sant'Anna*, Pisa, pp. 3-27

[25] Directorate General for the Information Society (2000) Commercial Exploitation of Europe's Public Sector Information: Final Report, pp. 8-14. Available online: http://ec.europa.eu/information_society/policy/psi/docs/pdfs/p ira_study/commercial_final_report.pdf (Last retrieved 05/07/2012)

[26] Murray-Rust, P. (2012) BioIT 2009 – What is data? *Personal blog on open knowledge.* Available online: http://blogs.ch.cam.ac.uk/pmr/2009/04/27/bioit-in-boston-what-is-open/ (Last retrieved 04/11/2012)

[27] Berners-Lee, T. (2010) Speech on "Open, Linked Data for a Global Community", *Gov 2.0 Expo 2010.* Available online: http://www.youtube.com/watch?feature=player_embedded&v=g a1aSJXCFe0 (Last retrieved 17/11/2012)

[28] EVPSI/LAPSI (2012) Web streaming of the 4th LAPSI Internal Conference and EVPSI/LAPSI Final Meeting (9th/10th July 2012). Retrieved from: http://www.lapsi-project.eu/streaming

[29] Murray-Rust, P. (2012) BioIT 2009 – What is data? *Personal blog on open knowledge.* Available online: http://blogs.ch.cam.ac.uk/pmr/2009/04/27/bioit-in-boston-what-is-open/ (Last retrieved 04/11/2012)

[30] Fioretti, M. (2011)" Open Data: Emerging trends, issues and best practices", *Laboratory of Economics and Management of Scuola*

69

Superiore Sant'Anna, Pisa, pp. 3-27

[31] Huijboom, N. & T. Van den Broek (2011) "Open data: an international comparison of strategies", *European Journal of ePractice,* 12 (March/April 2011), pp. 4-15. Available online: http://www.epractice.eu/files/European%20Journal%20epractice %20Volume%2012_4.pdf (Last retrieved 15/08/2012)

[32] Brown, G. (2010) Speech of the Prime Minister on Building Britain's Digital Future, London. Available online: http://webarchive.nationalarchives.gov.uk/+/number10.gov.uk/n ews/speeches-and-transcripts/2010/03/speech-on-building-britains-digital-future-22897 (Last retrieved 03/06/2012)

[33] Curtin, D.& A. Meijer (2006) "Does Transparency Strengthen Legitimacy? A Critical Analysis of European Union Policy Documents", *Information Polity,* 11(2006), pp. 109-122

[34] Fioretti, M. (2011)" Open Data: Emerging trends, issues and best practices", *Laboratory of Economics and Management of Scuola Superiore Sant'Anna,* Pisa, pp. 3-27

[35] Huijboom, N. & T. Van den Broek (2011) "Open data: an international comparison of strategies", *European Journal of ePractice,* 12 (March/April 2011), pp. 4-15. Available online: http://www.epractice.eu/files/European%20Journal%20epractice %20Volume%2012_4.pdf (Last retrieved 15/08/2012)

[36] Huijboom, N. & T. Van den Broek (2011) "Open data: an international comparison of strategies", *European Journal of ePractice,* 12 (March/April 2011), pp. 4-15. Available online: http://www.epractice.eu/files/European%20Journal%20epractice %20Volume%2012_4.pdf (Last retrieved 15/08/2012)

[37]O'Reilly, T. (2010) Government as a Platform, Lathrop, D. & L. Ruma (eds) *Open Government,* O'Reilly Media, p.11-44

[38] Group of authors (2010) Data, data, everywhere, *The Economist*, Special Report, Feb 25, 2010. Available online: http://www.economist.com/node/15557443 (Last retrieved 04/11/2012)

[39] Pentikousis, K. (2011) "Network Infrastructure at the Crossroads the Emergence of Smart Sities", Conference Publication on Intelligence in Next Generation Networks (ICIN), 15th International Conference, Berlin, 4-7 Oct. 2011.

[40] Fioretti, M. (2011)" Open Data: Emerging trends, issues and best practices", *Laboratory of Economics and Management of Scuola Superiore Sant'Anna*, Pisa, pp. 3-27

[41] Fioretti, M. (2011)" Open Data: Emerging trends, issues and best practices", *Laboratory of Economics and Management of Scuola Superiore Sant'Anna*, Pisa, pp. 13-23

[42] Dutra, M. (2011) Dangers of Open Government Data, *The Networked Society Blog*. Retrieved from: http://thenetworkedsociety.blogspot.be/2011/03/dangers-of-open-government-data.html (Last retrieved 04/11/2012)

[43] Fioretti, M. (2011)" Open Data: Emerging trends, issues and best practices", *Laboratory of Economics and Management of Scuola Superiore Sant'Anna*, Pisa, pp. 3-27

[44] Eaves, D. (2010) How Governments misunderstand the risks of Open Data, Personal Blog. Retrieved from: http://eaves.ca/2010/10/06/how-governments-misunderstand-the-risks-of-open-data/ (Last retrieved 04/11/2012)

[45] Fioretti, M. (2011)" Open Data: Emerging trends, issues and best practices", *Laboratory of Economics and Management of Scuola Superiore Sant'Anna*, Pisa, pp. 13-23

[46] Rogers, S. (2011) UK government open data: good bad or dangerous? Tell us what you think, *The Guardian Data Blog*. Available online: http://www.guardian.co.uk/news/datablog/2011/aug/04/uk-government-open-data-maude (Last retrieved 01/11/2012)

[47] Fioretti, M. (2011)" Open Data: Emerging trends, issues and best practices", *Laboratory of Economics and Management of Scuola Superiore Sant'Anna*, Pisa, pp. 3-27

[48] Huijboom, N. & T. Van den Broek (2011) "Open data: an international comparison of strategies", *European Journal of ePractice*, 12 (March/April 2011), pp. 4-15. Available online: http://www.epractice.eu/files/European%20Journal%20epractice%20Volume%2012_4.pdf (Last retrieved 15/08/2012)

[49] City of Hamilton (2011) Notice of Motion, *Open Data Policy*. Available online: http://www.hamilton.ca/NR/rdonlyres/E6C548DD-2FE2-4D21-AF65-B24A2C8BEF2B/0/Aug09EDRMS_n197439_v1_10_1__Notice_of_Motion__Open_Data_Polic.pdf (Last retrieved 01/11/2012)

[50] Uhlir, P.F. (2009) "The Socioeconomic Effects of Public Sector Information on Digital Networks: Toward a Better Understanding of Different Access and Reuse Policies: Workshop Summary", *US National Committee CODATA, in cooperation with OECD*, pp. 10-16.

[51] Huijboom, N. & T. Van den Broek (2011) "Open data: an international comparison of strategies", *European Journal of ePractice*, 12 (March/April 2011), pp. 4-15. Available online: http://www.epractice.eu/files/European%20Journal%20epractice%20Volume%2012_4.pdf (Last retrieved 15/08/2012)

[52] OECD (2004) "Declaration on Access to Research Data from Public Funding"

[53] OECD (2007) "Principles and Guidelines for Access to Research Data from Public Funding" Available online: http://www.oecd.org/science/scienceandtechnologypolicy/38500 813.pdf (Last retrieved 21/09/2012)

[54] OECD (2007) "Principles and Guidelines for Access to Research Data from Public Funding", p. 3. Available online: http://www.oecd.org/science/scienceandtechnologypolicy/38500 813.pdf (Last retrieved 21/09/2012)

[55] OECD (2007) "Principles and Guidelines for Access to Research Data from Public Funding", pp. 15-22. Available online: http://www.oecd.org/science/scienceandtechnologypolicy/38500 813.pdf (Last retrieved 21/09/2012)

[56] OECD (2007) "Principles and Guidelines for Access to Research Data from Public Funding", pp. 13-14. Available online: http://www.oecd.org/science/scienceandtechnologypolicy/38500 813.pdf (Last retrieved 21/09/2012)

[57] EUROPEAN COMMISSION. COM (2010) 245 final. Communication from the Commission to the European Parliament, the Council, the European Economic and Social Committee and the Committee of the Regions, a Digital Agenda for Europe. 19.5.2010. Available online: http://eur-lex.europa.eu/LexUriServ/LexUriServ.do?uri=COM:2010:0245:FI N:EN:PDF (Last retrieved 15/09/2012)

[58] EUROPEAN COMMISSION. COM (2010) 245 final. Communication from the Commission to the European Parliament, the Council, the European Economic and Social Committee and the Committee of the Regions, a Digital Agenda for Europe. 19.5.2010, p. 7. Available online: http://eur-lex.europa.eu/LexUriServ/LexUriServ.do?uri=COM:2010:0245:FI N:EN:PDF (Last retrieved 15/09/2012)

[59] Kroes, N. (2012) Speech on ePSI conference in Rotterdam March 2012. Available online: http://www.youtube.com/watch?v=9Jq4Qy1UeAE (Last retrieved 03/11/2012)

[60] EUROPEAN PARLIAMENT & COUNCIL (2003) DIRECTIVE 2003/98/EC OF THE EUROPEAN PARLIAMENT AND OF THE COUNCIL on the re-use of public sector information (of 17 November 2003), *Official Journal of the European Union* Available online: http://eur-lex.europa.eu/LexUriServ/LexUriServ.do?uri=OJ:L:2003:345:0090:0096:EN:PDF (Last retrieved 12/06/2012)

[61] EUROPEAN COMMISSION (2003) Proposal for a DIRECTIVE OF THE EUROPEAN PARLIAMENT AND OF THE COUNCIL, Amending Directive 2003/98/EC on re-use of public sector information Available online: http://ec.europa.eu/information_society/policy/psi/docs/pdfs/directive_proposal/2012/en.pdf (Last retrieved 08/06/2012)

[62] EUROPEAN PARLIAMENT & COUNCIL (2003) DIRECTIVE 2003/98/EC OF THE EUROPEAN PARLIAMENT AND OF THE COUNCIL on the re-use of public sector information (of 17 November 2003), *Official Journal of the European Union*, Article 2. Available online: http://eur-lex.europa.eu/LexUriServ/LexUriServ.do?uri=OJ:L:2003:345:0090:0096:EN:PDF (Last retrieved 12/06/2012)

[63] EUROPEAN PARLIAMENT & COUNCIL (2003) DIRECTIVE 2003/98/EC OF THE EUROPEAN PARLIAMENT AND OF THE COUNCIL on the re-use of public sector information (of 17 November 2003), *Official Journal of*

the European Union, Article 2. Available online: http://eur-lex.europa.eu/LexUriServ/LexUriServ.do?uri=OJ:L:2003:345:0090:0096:EN:PDF (Last retrieved 12/06/2012)

64 EUROPEAN PARLIAMENT & COUNCIL (2003) DIRECTIVE 2003/98/EC OF THE EUROPEAN PARLIAMENT AND OF THE COUNCIL on the re-use of public sector information (of 17 November 2003), *Official Journal of the European Union,* Article 6. Available online: http://eur-lex.europa.eu/LexUriServ/LexUriServ.do?uri=OJ:L:2003:345:0090:0096:EN:PDF (Last retrieved 12/06/2012)

65 EUROPEAN PARLIAMENT & COUNCIL (2003) DIRECTIVE 2003/98/EC OF THE EUROPEAN PARLIAMENT AND OF THE COUNCIL on the re-use of public sector information (of 17 November 2003), *Official Journal of the European Union,* Article 11. Available online: http://eur-lex.europa.eu/LexUriServ/LexUriServ.do?uri=OJ:L:2003:345:0090:0096:EN:PDF (Last retrieved 12/06/2012)

66 EUROPEAN PARLIAMENT & COUNCIL (2003) DIRECTIVE 2003/98/EC OF THE EUROPEAN PARLIAMENT AND OF THE COUNCIL on the re-use of public sector information (of 17 November 2003), *Official Journal of the European Union,* Article 3. Available online: http://eur-lex.europa.eu/LexUriServ/LexUriServ.do?uri=OJ:L:2003:345:0090:0096:EN:PDF (Last retrieved 12/06/2012)

67 Fornefeld, M. & G. Boele-Keimer, S. Recher, M. Fanning (2008) "Assessment of the Re-use of Public Sector Information (PSI) in the Geographical information, Meteorological Information and Legal Information Sectors", Final report, *MICUS Management Consulting GmbH,* Düsseldorf. Available online: http://ec.europa.eu/information_society/policy/psi/docs/pdfs/micus_report_december2008.pdf (Last retrieved 01/11/2012)

68 Fornefeld, M. & G. Boele-Keimer, S. Recher, M. Fanning (2008) "Assessment of the Re-use of Public Sector Information (PSI) in

the Geographical information, Meteorological Information and Legal Information Sectors", Final report, *MICUS Management Consulting GmbH*, Düsseldorf. Available online: http://ec.europa.eu/information_society/policy/psi/docs/pdfs/micus_report_december2008.pdf (Last retrieved 01/11/2012)

[69] EUROPEAN COMMISSION (2009) COMMUNICATION FROM THE COMMISSION TO THE EUROPEAN PARLIAMENT, THE COUNCIL, THE EUROPEAN ECONOMIC AND SOCIAL COMMITTEE AND THE COMMITTEE OF THE REGIONS Re-use of Public Sector Information – Review of Directive 2003/98/EC –2009/2011)

[70] Fornefeld, M. & G. Boele-Keimer, S. Recher, M. Fanning (2008) "Assessment of the Re-use of Public Sector Information (PSI) in the Geographical information, Meteorological Information and Legal Information Sectors", Final report, *MICUS Management Consulting GmbH*, Düsseldorf. Available online: http://ec.europa.eu/information_society/policy/psi/docs/pdfs/micus_report_december2008.pdf (Last retrieved 01/11/2012)

[71] Kronenburg, T. (2011) "Differences in the 2008 and 2010 public online consultations regarding the PSI Directive", Topic Report No. 2011/8, *European Public Sector Information Platform*. Available online: http://ru.scribd.com/doc/106896070/Topic-Report-Differences-Public-Consultations (Last retrieved 06/11/2012)

[72] EUROPEAN COMMISSION (2011) Legislative proposal 2011/0430(COD) - 12/12/2011. Available online: http://www.europarl.europa.eu/oeil/popups/summary.do?id=11 81131&t=d&l=en (Last retrieved 06/11/2012)

[73] EUROPEAN COMMISSION (2011) Legislative proposal

76

2011/0430(COD) - 12/12/2011. Available online: http://www.europarl.europa.eu/oeil/popups/summary.do?id=11 81131&t=d&l=en (Last retrieved 06/11/2012)

74 EUROPEAN COMMISSION (2003) Proposal for a DIRECTIVE OF THE EUROPEAN PARLIAMENT AND OF THE COUNCIL, Amending Directive 2003/98/EC on re-use of public sector information Available online: http://ec.europa.eu/information_society/policy/psi/docs/pdfs/d irective_proposal/2012/en.pdf (Last retrieved 08/06/2012)

75 EUROPEAN PARLIAMENT & COUNCIL (2007) DIRECTIVE 2007/2/EC OF THE EUROPEAN PARLIAMENT AND OF THE COUNCIL establishing an Infrastructure for Spatial Information in the European Community (INSPIRE) (of 14 March 2007), *Official Journal of the European Union*. Available online: http://eur-lex.europa.eu/LexUriServ/LexUriServ.do?uri=OJ:L:2007:108:0001 :0014:EN:PDF (Last retrieved 08/06/2012)

76 EUROPEAN PARLIAMENT & COUNCIL (2007) DIRECTIVE 2007/2/EC OF THE EUROPEAN PARLIAMENT AND OF THE COUNCIL establishing an Infrastructure for Spatial Information in the European Community (INSPIRE) (of 14 March 2007), *Official Journal of the European Union*, Article 2. Available online: http://eur-lex.europa.eu/LexUriServ/LexUriServ.do?uri=OJ:L:2007:108:0001 :0014:EN:PDF (Last retrieved 08/06/2012)

77 EUROPEAN PARLIAMENT & COUNCIL (2007) DIRECTIVE 2007/2/EC OF THE EUROPEAN PARLIAMENT AND OF THE COUNCIL establishing an

Infrastructure for Spatial Information in the European Community (INSPIRE) (of 14 March 2007), *Official Journal of the European Union*, *Annex* I,II,III. Available online: http://eur-lex.europa.eu/LexUriServ/LexUriServ.do?uri=OJ:L:2007:108:0001:0014:EN:PDF (Last retrieved 08/06/2012)

[78] EUROPEAN PARLIAMENT & COUNCIL (2007) DIRECTIVE 2007/2/EC OF THE EUROPEAN PARLIAMENT AND OF THE COUNCIL establishing an Infrastructure for Spatial Information in the European Community (INSPIRE) (of 14 March 2007), *Official Journal of the European Union*, Article 15. Available online: http://eur-lex.europa.eu/LexUriServ/LexUriServ.do?uri=OJ:L:2007:108:0001:0014:EN:PDF (Last retrieved 08/06/2012)

[79] EUROPEAN PARLIAMENT & COUNCIL (2007) DIRECTIVE 2007/2/EC OF THE EUROPEAN PARLIAMENT AND OF THE COUNCIL establishing an Infrastructure for Spatial Information in the European Community (INSPIRE) (of 14 March 2007), *Official Journal of the European Union*, Article 3. Available online: http://eur-lex.europa.eu/LexUriServ/LexUriServ.do?uri=OJ:L:2007:108:0001:0014:EN:PDF (Last retrieved 08/06/2012)

[80] EUROPEAN PARLIAMENT & COUNCIL (2007) DIRECTIVE 2007/2/EC OF THE EUROPEAN PARLIAMENT AND OF THE COUNCIL establishing an Infrastructure for Spatial Information in the European Community (INSPIRE) (of 14 March 2007), *Official Journal of the European Union*, Article 7. Available online: http://eur-lex.europa.eu/LexUriServ/LexUriServ.do?uri=OJ:L:2007:108:0001:0014:EN:PDF (Last retrieved 08/06/2012)

[81] EUROPEAN PARLIAMENT & COUNCIL (2007) DIRECTIVE 2007/2/EC OF THE EUROPEAN PARLIAMENT AND OF THE COUNCIL establishing an Infrastructure for Spatial Information in the European Community (INSPIRE) (of 14 March 2007), *Official Journal of the European Union*, Article 14. Available online: http://eur-lex.europa.eu/LexUriServ/LexUriServ.do?uri=OJ:L:2007:108:0001:0014:EN:PDF (Last retrieved 08/06/2012)

[82] EUROPEAN PARLIAMENT & COUNCIL (2007) DIRECTIVE 2007/2/EC OF THE EUROPEAN PARLIAMENT AND OF THE COUNCIL establishing an Infrastructure for Spatial Information in the European Community (INSPIRE) (of 14 March 2007), *Official Journal of the European Union*, Article 4. Available online: http://eur-lex.europa.eu/LexUriServ/LexUriServ.do?uri=OJ:L:2007:108:0001:0014:EN:PDF (Last retrieved 08/06/2012)